# Geography Activities

D129537

## HOLT

# World History
## The Human Journey

**HOLT, RINEHART AND WINSTON**

A Harcourt Education Company

**Austin** • Orlando • Chicago • New York • Toronto • London • San Diego

Weeks-Townsend Memorial Library
Union College
Barbourville, KY 40906

**Cover description:** Depiction of Charlemagne
**Cover credit:** Girandon/Art Resource

Copyright © by Holt, Rinehart and Winston

All rights reserved. No part of this publication may be reproduced or transmitted in any
form or by any means, electronic or mechanical, including photocopy, recording, or any
information storage and retrieval system, without permission in writing from the publisher.

Teachers using HOLT WORLD HISTORY: THE HUMAN JOURNEY may photocopy complete
pages in sufficient quantities for classroom use only and not for resale.

Printed in the United States of America

ISBN 0-03-065742-3

11  12  13  14 15  054  09 08 07 06

# Contents

## Geography Activities

Copyright © by Holt, Rinehart and Winston. All rights reserved.

Copyright © by Holt, Rinehart and Winston. All rights reserved.

Name _____ Class _____ Date _____

## The Emergence of Civilization

### ANTHROPOLOGY AND GEOLOGY

In 1911 a butterfly collector was chasing a butterfly in rural Tanganyika (now Tanzania) when he fell over the edge of a 300-foot cliff. The cliff turned out to be the edge of Olduvai Gorge. Scholars such as Mary and Louis Leakey, Donald Johanson, and Maurice Taieb later made many discoveries there about the evolution of humans. Most of the fossils at Olduvai Gorge have been found near the junction of the Main Gorge and the Side Gorge. The large map shows a view of the two gorges. The insert at the top shows a detailed view of the junction of the gorges. The insert at the bottom shows Olduvai Gorge in relation to surrounding geological features in northern Tanzania. Study the map below, and answer the questions that follow.

### Olduvai Gorge

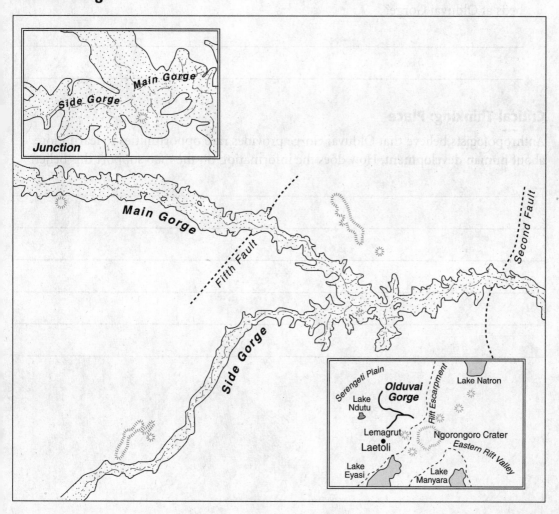

Copyright © by Holt, Rinehart and Winston. All rights reserved.

**Chapter 1, Geography Activity, continued**

**1.** In what plain does Olduvai Gorge lie?

_____

**2.** Where is Laetoli in relation to Olduvai Gorge?

_____

**3.** How might the earthquake faults around Olduvai Gorge affect fossil discoveries?

_____

_____

_____

**4.** How might Lemagrut, an extinct volcano, have affected the development of fossil beds at Olduvai Gorge?

_____

_____

## Critical Thinking: Place

Anthropologists believe that Olduvai Gorge provides rare opportunities to learn more about human development. How does the information on the map support this belief?

_____

_____

_____

_____

_____

Copyright © by Holt, Rinehart and Winston. All rights reserved.

Name _____ Class _____ Date _____

Geography Activity

## The First Civilizations

## THE END OF AN ISLAND CIVILIZATION

Crete rose to the center of the thriving Minoan civilization due in large part to geographic factors. Crete's position as a large island with many island neighbors made it a natural shipping center. So did its location between Europe and the great civilizations of Asia Minor. The people of Crete built a massive shipping fleet to handle trade between the two areas.

Crete's fertile soil and mild climate made it self-sufficient in food production. Its population turned to developing crafts, trading goods, and administering the powerful Minoan civilization.

Despite all these advantages, Crete and the Minoans lost their power suddenly. For centuries, historians wondered why. Only recently have archaeological and geological finds in the Aegean and Mediterranean seas offered a possible explanation. It now appears that Crete was badly damaged as a result of volcanic activity on Thera (now called Santorini), an island in the Aegean Sea.

Archaeological evidence showed that sometime between 1500 and 1400 B.C., many towns in Crete were destroyed. Geologists found a thick layer of volcanic ash buried deep in the sediment below the Aegean and Mediterranean seas. This layer was estimated to have been there since about 1450 B.C. Finally, the remains of a Minoan town were found on Thera. The town had been destroyed by a volcano and buried under volcanic ash.

Further study showed that one of the most powerful volcanic eruptions ever known had occurred on Thera about 1450 B.C. The force of the volcano had literally blown the top off the island. It sent rock and ash 20 miles into the atmosphere. The eruption opened a huge crater 6 miles wide and 2,500 feet deep.

Thera was transformed from one island into five. Sea water rushed in to fill the crater. This massive displacement of water created huge waves that raced toward the north shore of Crete. The waves also washed the shores of all the islands of the Aegean and even touched the Mediterranean coast. The ash and debris hitting the atmosphere moved east and southeast from Thera. Volcanic dust blanketed a wide area.

## Crete and the Aegean

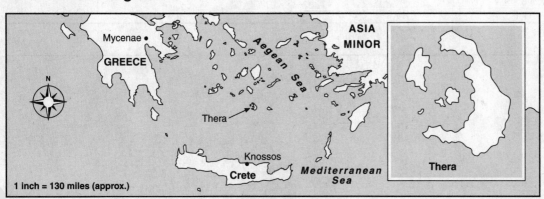

1 inch = 130 miles (approx.)

Copyright © by Holt, Rinehart and Winston. All rights reserved.

Chapter 2, Geography Activity, continued

Geologists theorize that the waves destroyed the Cretan fleet and flooded the land. Volcanic dust covered the eastern half of the island and destroyed crops. Such a catastrophe must have weakened the entire Aegean area. It probably also left the Minoans easy targets for attack. Study the map on page 3, and answer the questions that follow.

1. What physical features does Crete have that would have encouraged the building of a large fleet of ships?

_____

_____

2. How far does Crete stretch from east to west?

_____

3. How far is Crete from Thera? (Note that Thera is indicated by an arrow on the map.)

_____

4. Look at the inset map of Thera on the previous page. What do you think the island looked like before the volcanic eruption?

_____

_____

## Critical Thinking: Human-Environment Interaction

How could the volcanic eruption on Thera have destroyed crops on Crete? What does this suggest about the other environmental changes in the Aegean and Mediterranean and their effects on human settlements?

_____

_____

_____

_____

Copyright © by Holt, Rinehart and Winston. All rights reserved.

# CHAPTER 3

## Geography Activity

### Ancient Indian Civilizations

**INDIAN TRADE**

Around 2500 B.C. a civilization began to develop around the Indus River in what is now Pakistan and western India. In addition to the cities of Mohenjo-Daro and Harappa, archaeologists have uncovered many other sites along the Indus River valley that were part of the Harappan civilization. Ruins of ancient cities show that those ancient people built drainage systems that ran into brick-lined sewers. Brick homes many stories high were common. They also developed systems of writing and counting and dug canals to irrigate their farms. The port of Lothal, for example, had an enclosed shipping dock that was more than 700 feet long. There also was a sluice gate that made it possible to load ships at high or low tide. At such ports, Harappans exported gold, copper, lapis lazuli, turquoise, timber, ivory and cotton. Examine the map below and answer the questions that follow.

**Regional Map of India**

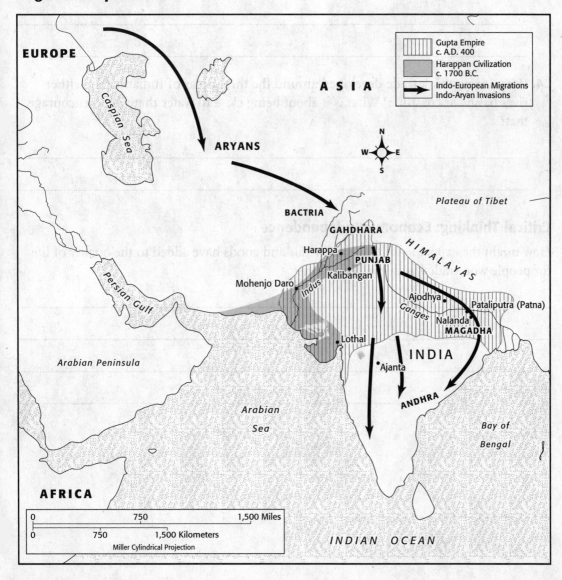

Copyright © by Holt, Rinehart and Winston. All rights reserved.

**1.** Trade occurred between the inhabitants of the cities of Harappa and Mohenjo-Daro. What were some of the items exchanged between occupants of these two cities of the Harappan civilization?

_____

_____

**2.** Why do you think trade first developed in the southern region along the coast?

_____

_____

**3.** What type of economic activity do you think took place in the city of Lothal, and why?

_____

_____

**4.** Why do you think trade developed around the three areas of India that are either river basins or coastline? What is it about being close to water that would encourage that?

_____

_____

## Critical Thinking: Economic Independence

How might the exporting of valuable metals and goods have added to the quality of life for people who traded with the Harappans?

_____

_____

_____

_____

Copyright © by Holt, Rinehart and Winston. All rights reserved.

**CHAPTER 4**

Geography Activity

## Ancient Chinese Civilization

## POLITICAL TURMOIL IN CHINA

By the early 400s B.C., many Chinese leaders had lost confidence in diplomacy as a means of resolving disputes. Several states emerged as leading powers. They battled each other for dominance. By the end of the Era of Warring States, the Qin state had triumphed over the others. Examine the map below, and answer the questions that follow.

**The Warring States**

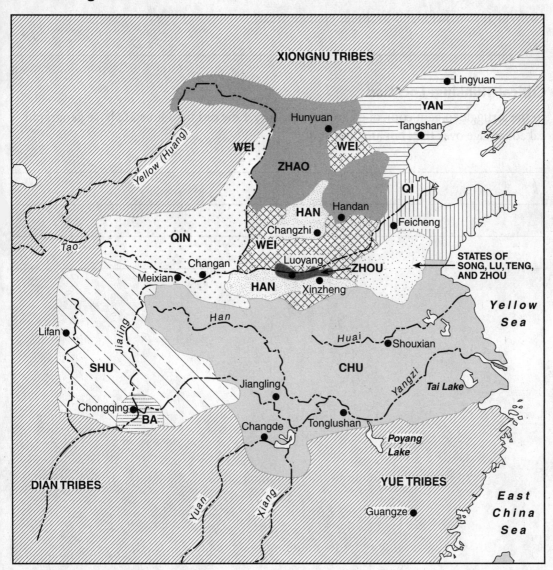

Copyright © by Holt, Rinehart and Winston. All rights reserved.

Name _____ Class _____ Date _____

Chapter 4, Geography Activity, continued

**1.** Which state controlled the most territory?

_____

**2.** Which states had direct access to the Yellow Sea?

_____

**3.** Which state controlled the cities of Lingyuan and Tangshan?

_____

**4.** Which state held land in three separate areas?

_____

## Critical Thinking: Location

In the struggle to gain control of greater territory, how did the Qin state have geographical advantage over the Han and Wei states?

_____

_____

_____

_____

Copyright © by Holt, Rinehart and Winston. All rights reserved.

Name _____ Class _____ Date _____

## The Greek City-States

### GREEK ALLIANCES

In the years following the Persian Wars, many Greek city-states banded together for mutual protection. Two main alliances developed: the Delian League and the Spartan confederacy. Increasingly, Athens gained control over the Delian League until the alliance was essentially an Athenian empire. Study the map below and answer the questions that follow.

### Athenian Empire, 440 B.C.

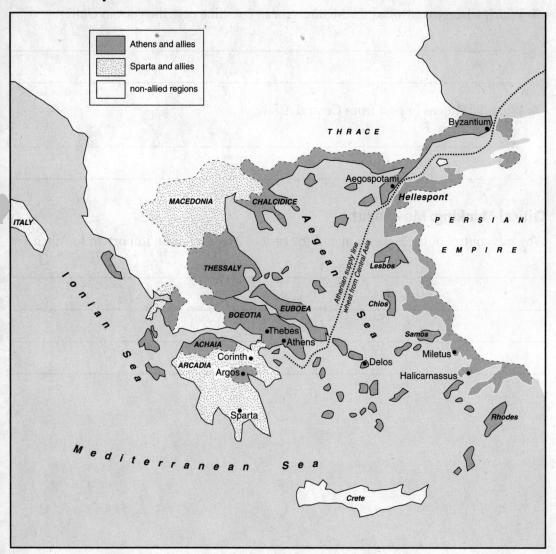

**Chapter 5, Geography Activity, continued**

**1.** What regions were allied with Athens?

_____

_____

**2.** What regions were allied with Sparta?

_____

_____

**3.** Which alliance controlled the Mediterranean coastline near the Persian Gulf?

_____

_____

**4.** What did Athens import from Central Asia?

_____

_____

## Critical Thinking: Movement

Why was control of the Hellespont and the eastern Mediterranean important to Athens?

_____

_____

_____

_____

Copyright © by Holt, Rinehart and Winston. All rights reserved.

## CHAPTER 6

Geography Activity

### Greece's Golden and Hellenistic Ages

**STOPPING ALEXANDER THE GREAT**

During their long march eastward toward the Indus River, Alexander the Great and his army met and overcame many enemies. The most difficult enemies to overcome, however, seemed to come from nature itself. Perhaps the most difficult barrier was the Hindu Kush, the mountain range whose name means "Killer of the Hindus." These mountains are located in what is now northeastern Afghanistan, Pakistan, and northwestern India.

In December of 328 B.C., the snow-covered Hindu Kush blocked Alexander's path. He had to wait until spring to lead his men single file through the narrow Khawak pass, which was 11,650 feet high. The brave troops faced a winding climb and descent. Nevertheless, the troops pushed on until they reached the Indus River a year later. There they faced not only a large, well-equipped army, but also drenching monsoon rains.

Monsoons are seasonal winds that blow over the Indian Ocean and the land that surrounds it. They are created as a result of the difference in temperature over land and sea. In the spring, the sun's rays fall more directly on the earth. The land heats up and the air over it becomes hot and dry. The ocean does not warm as quickly, so the air above it remains cooler and more moist. The warm, dry air rises high above the land, creating low atmospheric pressure. The difference in pressure created by the rising air pulls the cooler, moist air from the southwest, creating monsoon winds. These winds bring torrential rains with them. The summer rainy season lasts from mid-June to mid-September.

In the fall, the land begins to cool more quickly than the sea, and the reverse situation occurs. Now the cool air over the land rushes out to replace the rising warm air over the sea. This brings on the winter dry season.

Alexander must not have known about such harsh climate conditions, because he started his attack as the monsoon rains began. His men fought on, creating bridges of boats to cross swollen rivers. Although Alexander's forces were victorious, they had had enough. The unending rains had destroyed their weapons and food, and forced them to live in constantly wet uniforms. Just as Alexander's forces reached the point where India lay before them for the taking, they refused to go on. The monsoons and the mutiny ended Alexander's eastward march, and he began the long journey home. Study the map and answer the questions that follow.

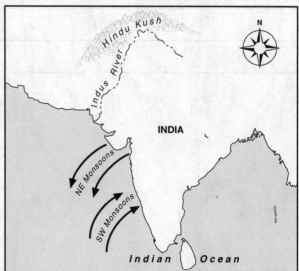

**India and the Monsoons**

Copyright © by Holt, Rinehart and Winston. All rights reserved.

## Chapter 6, Geography Activity, continued

**1.** From what direction did Alexander attempt to invade India?

_____

_____

**2.** What geographical feature complicated Alexander's assault on India?

_____

_____

_____

**3.** How did climate affect Alexander's assault on India?

_____

_____

_____

**4.** Did Alexander's army encounter the southwest monsoons or the northeast monsoons?

_____

_____

## Critical Thinking: Movement

Discuss how advance knowledge of the monsoons might have influenced Alexander's plans to invade India.

_____

_____

_____

_____

Copyright © by Holt, Rinehart and Winston. All rights reserved.

# CHAPTER 7

## Geography Activity

### The Roman World

## THE ROME OF AUGUSTUS

During his reign (27 B.C.–A.D. 14) Augustus worked to transform Rome. He established a police force and fire brigade and built and restored several aqueducts. He also oversaw construction of many buildings throughout the city. In addition, he had the surfaces of many existing buildings overlaid with marble to improve their appearance and make them more impressive. The map below shows Rome during Augustus's reign. Study the map, and answer the questions that follow.

## The City of Rome

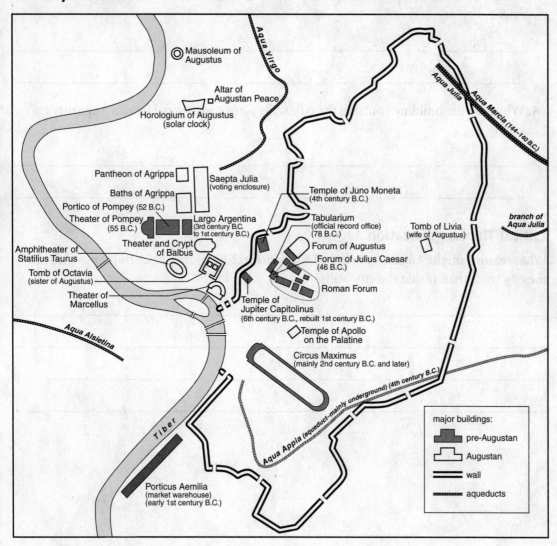

Chapter 7, Geography Activity, continued

1. Which temple was constructed during Augustus's reign?

_____

_____

2. What building is located southwest of the city walls?

_____

_____

3. Which of the buildings inside the city walls were constructed during Augustus's reign?

_____

_____

4. Which of the buildings outside the city walls were constructed before Augustus's reign?

_____

_____

## Critical Thinking: Location

What reasons might Augustus have had for constructing more public buildings outside the city walls than inside the city walls?

_____

_____

_____

_____

Copyright © by Holt, Rinehart and Winston. All rights reserved.

Name _____ Class _____ Date _____

# Geography Activity
## Africa

## THE SPREAD OF IRONWORKING

Geographical isolation, climate differences, and geographic diversity were three critical factors in shaping the cultures of the vast continent of Africa. In East Africa, settlers spread down the Rift Valley from Ethiopia. Of further importance, trans-Saharan trade increased after 100 B.C. with the introduction of the domestic camel from Asia. These developments aided the spread of iron tools and weapons, which had been introduced by the Greeks and Carthaginians in the 700s and 600s B.C. Study the map below and answer the questions that follow.

## Ironworking in Africa

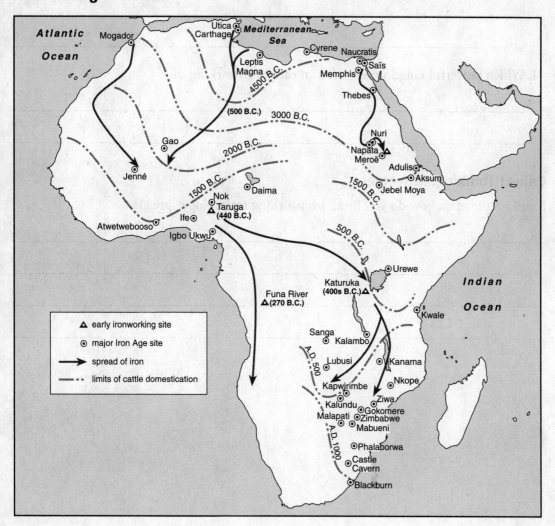

Copyright © by Holt, Rinehart and Winston. All rights reserved.

**Chapter 8, Geography Activity, continued**

1. In which areas in Africa was iron technology first introduced?

   _____

   _____

2. In which direction did iron technology spread?

   _____

   _____

3. What accompanied the introduction of ironworking?

   _____

   _____

4. Which powerful kingdom was also an early ironworking site?

   _____

   _____

**Critical Thinking: Movement**

Based on the map, how do you think ironworking technology spread?

_____

_____

_____

_____

Copyright © by Holt, Rinehart and Winston. All rights reserved.

## CHAPTER 9

Geography Activity

### The Americas

**THE MAYA EMPIRE**

The Yucatán Peninsula was home to the Maya. The Maya people built elaborate cities throughout their territory. These cities contained temples, ball courts, sacrificial wells, and astronomical observatories. Study the map below and answer the questions that follow.

## Maya Cities in the Yucatán

**Chapter 9, Geography Activity, continued**

**1.** Which Maya settlement do you think would have been most threatened by hurricanes? Why?

_____

_____

**2.** Which Maya site is the farthest west?

_____

_____

**3.** About how far was Chichén Itzá from Uxmal?

_____

_____

**4.** Which cities were located in marshy zones?

_____

_____

## Critical Thinking: Place

How do you think altitude influenced the establishment of Maya cities?

_____

_____

_____

_____

Copyright © by Holt, Rinehart and Winston. All rights reserved.

# CHAPTER 10 — Geography Activity

Modern Chapter 1

## The Byzantine Empire and Russia

### CONSTANTINOPLE—CROSSROADS OF EUROPE AND ASIA

About 650 B.C. a Greek named Byzas wanted to establish a new Greek colony. He consulted the oracle at Delphi for advice on where to locate his settlement. Byzas was told to establish a city "opposite the blind." He took this to mean "blind people." Searching for a site, Byzas reached the Bosporus. This strait is 20 miles long and 2,000 feet wide. It separates Europe from Asia and connects the Black Sea and the Sea of Marmara.

Byzas noted that a Greek colony, Chalcedon, had already been established on the Asian side of the Bosporus. He felt, however, that the European side was far superior. Here, seven hills rise above the waters of the Bosporus. An inlet creates a natural harbor. Byzas believed that the people of Chalcedon must have been blind not to recognize this geographic advantage. He realized then that he had found his site "opposite the blind." Byzas' city, Byzantium, was soon established on the European shore.

Byzantium prospered immediately, thanks to its commanding geographic position. It collected tolls from those who sailed beneath the city walls through the Bosporus. It made the most of its location and became an important trading center. As artisans opened busy shops, the city also became a major producer of goods.

It is no wonder that the Emperor Constantine chose Byzantium to be the capital of the Eastern Roman Empire in A.D. 330. He was attracted by its location on a peninsula that could be fortified. Also the city's location assured its control of the navigation through the Bosporus from the Black Sea to the Aegean and Mediterranean seas. Constantine wanted to make Byzantium a capital worthy of a great empire. He ordered the building of more walls around the city. This would make it, he thought, an "impregnable fortress enclosing the sea." He also gave Byzantium a new name in his honor—Constantinople.

By the 900s, Constantinople had become one of the world's largest cities. Located at the crossroads of the world, Constantinople was subject to attack from both east and west. The inhabitants therefore mounted bronze tubes on the walls of the city. When Constantinople was under attack, a substance called "Greek fire" was poured down the tubes onto the invaders. This devastating weapon was a flammable mixture of sulfur, naptha, and quicklime. When ignited, it became liquid fire. Constantinople was able to defeat all invaders until 1204. Study the map, and answer the questions that follow.

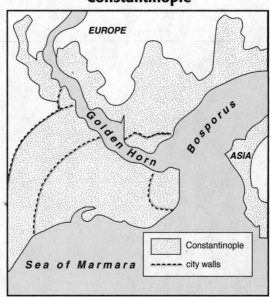

Constantinople

Copyright © by Holt, Rinehart and Winston. All rights reserved.

## Chapter 10, Geography Activity, continued

1. What geographic features made Constantinople highly defensible?

   _____

   _____

2. What is the name of the inlet that helps to form Constantinople's natural harbor?

   _____

   _____

3. Through what strait would ships have to pass after leaving Byzantium for the Mediterranean?

   _____

   _____

4. What information on the map indicates that the city expanded over time?

   _____

   _____

## Critical Thinking: Location

How did Constantinople's location make it a "crossroads of Europe and Asia"?

_____

_____

_____

_____

Copyright © by Holt, Rinehart and Winston. All rights reserved.

# CHAPTER  11

## Modern Chapter 2

# Geography Activity

## The Islamic World

### THE SPREAD OF ISLAM

Islamic culture spread quickly. This was due in part to the extensive trade networks that connected the Arabian Peninsula to Asia and Africa. Beginning in the 1200s, Muslims began to make inroads into Southeast Asia. By the 1500s many people—from Sumatra to the Philippines—had converted to Islam. Study the map below, and answer the questions that follow.

### Islam in Southeast Asia

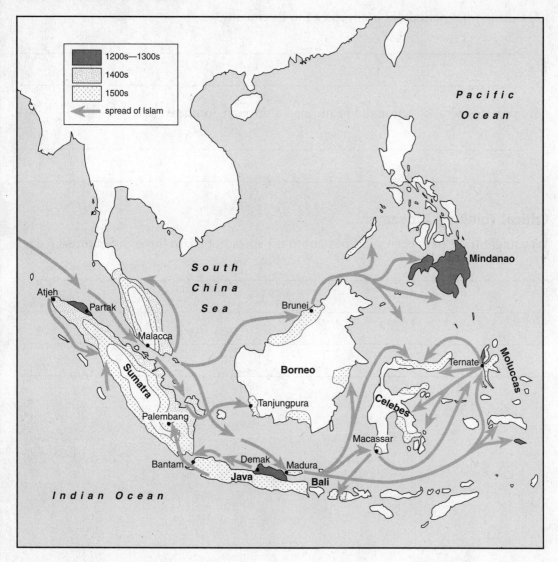

Copyright © by Holt, Rinehart and Winston. All rights reserved.

## Chapter 11, Geography Activity, continued

**1.** Which areas showed Muslim influence between the 1200s and the 1300s?

_____

_____

**2.** Which island was influenced by Islam first: Borneo or Mindanao?

_____

_____

**3.** During what period did Islam spread to Palembang?

_____

_____

**4.** In what general direction did Islam spread through Southeast Asia?

_____

_____

## Critical Thinking: Movement

Why might trade have been so important to the spread of Islam through Southeast Asia?

_____

_____

_____

_____

Copyright © by Holt, Rinehart and Winston. All rights reserved.

# CHAPTER 12

Modern Chapter **3**

## Geography Activity

## The Civilizations of East Asia

### THE WIND THAT SAVED JAPAN

In the late 1200s, Kublai Khan ruled the mighty Mongol Empire, which stretched from the Black Sea to the South China Sea. He had completed the Mongol conquest of China and extended Mongol rule to Korea. Next he tried to conquer Japan.

In 1274 Kublai Khan sailed for Japan from Korea with a force of 900 ships and 40,000 men. In November the force sailed into Hakata Bay on the island of Kyushu. After a day's fighting, the Mongols returned to their ships, intent on renewing the attack the following day. That night, however, a fierce storm drove the Mongol force out to sea. There, mighty winds sank 200 ships with the loss of 13,500 lives. The severely weakened Mongol force returned to the Asia mainland.

The great Khan was disappointed, but he was not discouraged. Once again he began to assemble an attack force. In his eagerness to control Japan, however, Kublai Khan had failed to learn an important lesson from the disaster in 1274. The storm that fateful night had not been an unusual event. From July through November, such storms are not uncommon in the western Pacific Ocean. At that time of year, devastating storms called typhoons form over water in the trade winds latitudes—between 0° and 30° north and south of the equator.

A typhoon consists of winds reaching 100 to 150 miles an hour that swirl around a storm center. Within this "eye" of the storm, all is clear and calm. But the ranging winds around the "eye" send out a destructive force ranging from over 50 to 200 miles. While in the trade winds latitude, a typhoon travels in a northwesterly direction. Then it turns and travels in a northeasterly direction.

### Typhoons in Asia

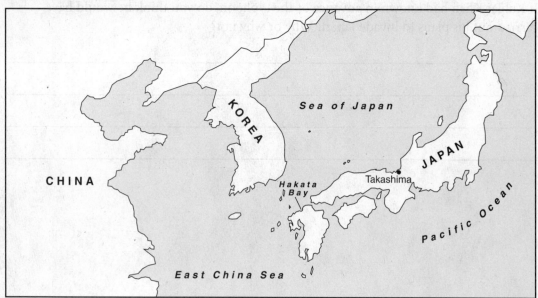

Copyright © by Holt, Rinehart and Winston. All rights reserved.

Name _____ Class _____ Date _____

It was during the typhoon season of 1281 that Kublai Khan's forces attacked Japan again. One force of 900 ships and 42,000 men left from Korea; 3,500 ships and 100,000 men sailed from China. The two forces met at Takashima in July, ready to attack Kyushu.

Once again nature proved to be a powerful enemy of the Mongols. In August a typhoon turned toward Kyushu. Here it passed through the invasion force, creating a great destruction. The Mongols lost an estimated 4,000 ships and 10,000 men. To the Japanese, the typhoon was a heaven-sent "divine wind" or *kamikaze,* saving them from Mongol domination. Study the map on page 23, and answer the questions that follow.

**1.** On the map, draw the probable paths followed by the two invasion forces in 1281.

_____

_____

**2.** On the map, draw the probable path of the typhoon passing over Japan.

_____

_____

**3.** How did the Japanese explain the great storms that destroyed both Mongol forces?

_____

_____

## Critical Thinking: Human-Environment Interaction

If Kublai Khan had known in advance of the typhoon, do you think he would have carried out his plans to invade Japan? Why or why not?

_____

_____

_____

_____

Copyright © by Holt, Rinehart and Winston. All rights reserved.

## CHAPTER 13

Modern Chapter 4

# Geography Activity

## The Rise of the Middle Ages

### ENGLAND UNDER THE NORMANS

Norman rule in England began when William of Normandy—also known as William the Conqueror— invaded England in 1066 and conquered the Saxons. Many historians believe that William's greatest legacy is the Domesday Book. This survey of his new realm told William how much land he owned, how other lands were divided, and who lived upon the land. It also contained information on the material and financial resources of his subjects. In order to survey England, the country was divided into districts. Each district provided census takers who were familiar with the region. Normans and Saxons alike were surveyed. Many English families today trace their names to entries in the Domesday Book. Study the map below and answer the questions that follow.

### The Domesday Book, 1086

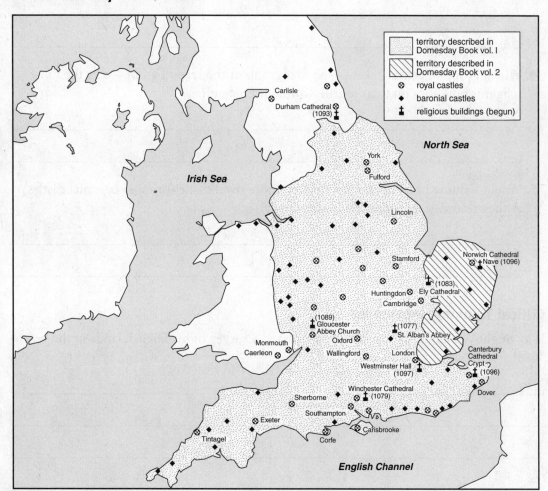

Copyright © by Holt, Rinehart and Winston. All rights reserved.

## Chapter 13, Geography Activity, continued

**1.** Was William's survey begun in the region that included Winchester Cathedral, or in the region that included Norwich Cathedral Nave?

_____

_____

**2.** Were census takers first sent to central England, or to lands along the eastern coast?

_____

_____

**3.** How many baronial castles were surveyed in the second volume of the Domesday Book?

_____

_____

**4.** Which group of census takers—the first group or the second group—saw the most religious buildings on their journey through England?

_____

_____

**5.** Would Volume I census takers have seen more royal castles or more baronial castles as they recorded their portion of the survey?

_____

_____

## Critical Thinking: Movement

Why might William of Normandy have ordered a survey of his English lands in the year 1086?

_____

_____

_____

_____

Copyright © by Holt, Rinehart and Winston. All rights reserved.

# CHAPTER 14

Modern Chapter 5

## Geography Activity

## The High Middle Ages

## THE BLACK DEATH DEVASTATES EUROPE

Europe went through a period of economic and population growth from the early 1100s to the 1340s. Then came a staggering blow that not only stopped this progress but also sent Europe into a tragic decline. Europe would not even begin to recover for more than 100 years.

It began in 1347 when a merchant ship set sail from a port on the Black Sea with a cargo of goods bound for Genoa, Italy. On board were rats infected with bacteria that could strike in different forms. One form was bubonic plague. Transmitted to humans by fleas on the infected rats, it attacked the glands and caused swelling and high fever. Another form was pneumonic plague. Transmitted by an infected person to other people, it attacked the lungs. Either form was generally fatal within three or four days.

By 1348 the plague, now called the Black Death, raged in Italy and was carried on trading routes to France and Spain. By 1349 it had swept into the Holy Roman Empire, Hungary, and England. By 1350 it reached Poland and Russia.

The death rates were devasting—so devastating that today's historians still do not know how many people actually died. Record keeping was abandoned in the face of such disaster. Italy is thought to have lost most of its population and England, one-third. Estimates are that one-fourth to one-third of Europe's population died during the height of the plague from 1348 to 1351. Worldwide, the figure might have been 75 million during this period. It may have been the largest loss of human life of any catastrophe in history.

Renewed outbreaks of plague made population growth impossible until the late 1400s. Human population recovery finally became noticeable in the 1470s and 1480s. In the 1500s, population actually boomed, finally recovering the losses suffered from the Black Death.

## The Black Death

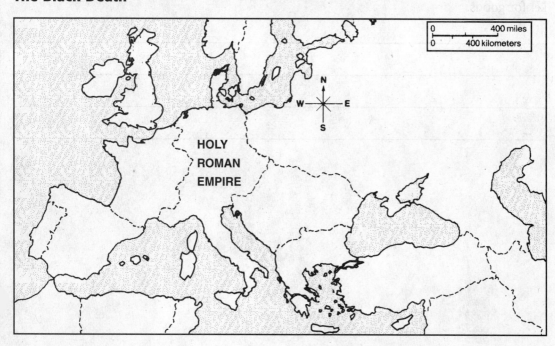

Copyright © by Holt, Rinehart and Winston. All rights reserved.

Chapter 14, Geography Activity, *continued*

**1.** What are the major bodies of water shown on the map? Label them on the map.

_____

_____

**2.** What areas of Europe were struck by the plague? Label and color these in on the map.

_____

_____

**3.** What was the probable trade route used by the ship that first brought the plague bacteria from the Black Sea? Label this trade route on the map.

_____

_____

**4.** Draw an arrow on the map showing the route the plague followed through Europe. Enter dates for the years it reached each area on the map.

_____

_____

## Critical Thinking: Economics

What do you think happened to the economies of the countries afflicted by the Black Death? Explain your answer in terms of economic growth, the labor force, and the market for goods.

_____

_____

_____

_____

Copyright © by Holt, Rinehart and Winston. All rights reserved.

Name _____ Class _____ Date _____

# CHAPTER 15

Modern Chapter **6**

Geography Activity

## The Renaissance and Reformation

## THE SPREAD OF THE RENAISSANCE AND REFORMATION

During the 1100s and 1200s, the Italian cities of Florence, Milan, Venice, and Ferrara developed into thriving urban areas. Merchants during this time controlled commerce and finance across Europe from these Italian cities. They used them as home bases for developing commercial activity such as banking and lending.

The beginning of the Renaissance is said to have occurred in Italy during the 1300s. During this period, the agricultural economy developed into a commercial economy. This new economy featured trade and the selling of goods. Political institutions were created to address the needs of the urban areas. This marked a change from reliance on the church for these things. The common person began to take an interest in the arts, literature, and music. These had only been available to religious intellectuals prior to this time.

## Europe after the Reformation

Copyright © by Holt, Rinehart and Winston. All rights reserved.

## Chapter 15, Geography Activity, continued

The printing press, developed around 1450, was one of the most important inventions of the time. It helped to spread the ideas of the Renaissance. Before the printing press, books were created mostly by monks who wrote them one by one. Now common villagers became consumers of the news and information that affected their everyday lives. Although most villagers could not read, the availability of the printed material increased the literacy rate among them. It also led to a greater desire for more and better information.

As a result of this increased communication, the Reformation occurred at the same time as the Renaissance. The Reformation can be described as a revolt by people throughout Europe against the Catholic Church. After the Reformation, religious organizations such as the Protestants, Lutherans, Calvinists, and Anglicans formed. These organizations challenged the teachings of the Catholic Church. This challenge from the outside led to reforms within the Catholic Church. This movement is known as the Counter-Reformation.

The overall result of this religious, intellectual, and political upheaval was a decrease in the influence of the church and an increase in individualism in the everyday lives of the people of Europe. Examine the map on page 29 and answer the questions that follow.

**1.** Why did the uprising against the Catholic Church occur throughout Europe?

_____

_____

**2.** In what countries did the Roman Catholic Church remain the major religion?

_____

_____

**3.** What was the major religion in Iceland, Norway, and Sweden?

_____

_____

## Critical Thinking: Human Interaction

How did the printing press bring new information and ideas to people?

_____

_____

_____

Copyright © by Holt, Rinehart and Winston. All rights reserved.

# CHAPTER 16

Modern Chapter 7

## Geography Activity

## Exploration and Expansion

### CROSSING THE ATLANTIC

Christopher Columbus first thought about the possibility of reaching India by sailing west while working as a chart maker in Lisbon, Portugal. Columbus, an Italian navigator, had gone to Lisbon after being shipwrecked off the Portuguese coast in 1476. While in Portugal he was in constant contact with ships' pilots and navigators. These seafarers believed that islands existed west of the European continent. Columbus thought that they must be about 2,500 miles west of Europe.

Columbus's own sailing experience, and the information he had gathered from other sailors, gave him a great deal of information about wind directions and ocean currents. By using this knowledge properly, he believed he could safely reach India by sailing west.

Columbus first took his plan to King John II of Portugal in 1484. However, the king was not interested in financing it. He felt that Columbus was underestimating the distance involved. Moreover, King John was backing explorations to find a sea route to India around the tip of Africa. Disappointed, Columbus went to Isabella and Ferdinand of Spain, but they were involved with expelling Muslims from Spain. In 1488 Columbus returned to Lisbon to petition King John again. As he did, word came that Bartolomeu Dias had successfully sailed around the Cape of Good Hope at the southern tip of Africa. That ended any possible Portuguese interest in Columbus's plan. Once more, Columbus went to the Spanish royal court. Finally, in April 1492, he received word of Isabella and Ferdinand's support.

At last, after eight years of presenting his plan to anyone who would listen, Columbus set sail. He headed first for the Canary Islands and from there he sailed due west. Study the map below, and answer the questions that follow.

### Crossing the Atlantic

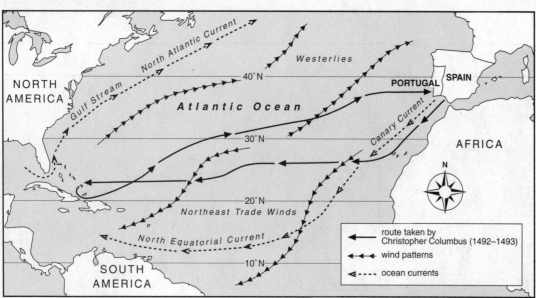

**Chapter 16, Geography Activity, continued**

**1.** What ocean currents would have helped Columbus on his journey westward?

_____

_____

**2.** What winds would have helped Columbus sail westward?

_____

_____

**3.** What ocean currents would have helped Columbus on the return trip to Europe?

_____

_____

**4.** What winds would have helped on the return trip?

_____

_____

## Critical Thinking: Movement

Why would Columbus have taken the slightly northward and southward routes shown on the map, rather than sailing on a straight path?

_____

_____

_____

_____

Copyright © by Holt, Rinehart and Winston. All rights reserved.

# CHAPTER **17**        Geography Activity

Modern Chapter **8**                                **Asia in Transition**

## THE STRUGGLE FOR KOREA

The Mongols invaded Korea in 1231, launching a series of wars that ended with their conquest of Koryo, the northernmost state in Korea at that time. Koryo was able to drive out the Mongols in 1356, but the state was in disarray and ended in 1392.

Korea next came under the influence of Yi Songgye. His belief in neo-Confucianism, Taoism, and Buddhism allowed for social and political reform and relative peace in the region for nearly 200 years. This ultimately led to the founding of the Chosŏn Dynasty in Korea in the 1300s.

Chosŏn was invaded in 1592 by the Japanese, who wanted to use Korea as a stepping stone to invade China. By 1598, however, Chosŏn had repulsed the Japanese, with the aid of China's Ming Dynasty and the efforts of its own naval hero, Yi Sunsin. Korea was invaded twice by the Manchus in 1627 and 1636. The Manchu conquest of China in 1644 caused problems in Chosŏn. However, it also allowed the Koreans to create their own identity during this period free from Chinese influence.

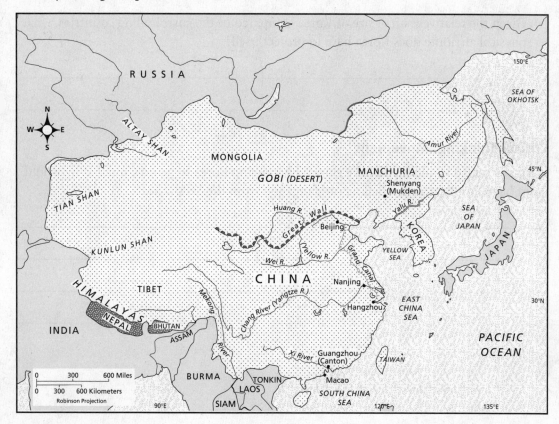

Copyright © by Holt, Rinehart and Winston. All rights reserved.

**Chapter 17, Geography Activity, continued**

1. How has the water that forms most of Korea's borders helped the country to defend itself from attack?

   _____

   _____

   _____

2. Why would the Manchus have had an easier time invading China than Korea?

   _____

   _____

   _____

3. Between the 1100s and 1300s, how many times was Korea invaded from the north?

   _____

   _____

   _____

4. Given the relatively small size of Korea compared to the surrounding countries, what physical attribute does Korea have to protect itself?

   _____

   _____

   _____

## Critical Thinking: Movement

What advantage would Japan have gained by crossing Korea to get to China? Why would it not have simply attacked Beijing or Hangzhou from the Yellow Sea?

_____

_____

_____

_____

Copyright © by Holt, Rinehart and Winston. All rights reserved.

# CHAPTER 18

Modern Chapter **9**

Geography Activity

**Islamic Empires in Asia**

## ISLAM AND TRADE

The Safavid Empire developed economically during the reign of Shah ʿAbbās the Great. Several things combined to make that happen. First, ʿAbbās changed the capital of the Safavid Empire from Tabrīz to Eṣfahān. Secondly, the Shah encouraged manufacturing and foreign trade. Carpets and Persian rugs were traded to Europe, where they were sold to wealthy Europeans. Persian merchants also exported fabrics such as silk, brocade, and damask to Europe. They also manufactured tile and ceramics for trade to Europe and use throughout the empire.

After the decline of the Safavid Empire, the Mughal Empire continued the Islamic trade tradition. Because the Mughal Empire was located along the sea routes to Asia, it was able to export large quantities of jewels and gold. Examine the map below, and answer the questions that follow.

## The Safavid Empire

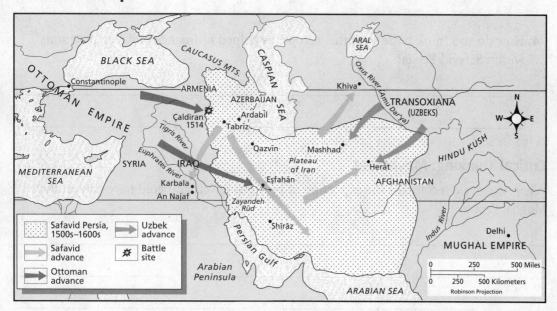

Copyright © by Holt, Rinehart and Winston. All rights reserved.

**1.** What role did Shah 'Abbās the Great have in making Eşfahān the commercial capital of the Islamic world?

_____

_____

**2.** Why would bringing exotic and rich fabrics to Europe increase the commercial value of the Safavid Empire?

_____

_____

**3.** How would locating major cities by sea routes increase trade?

_____

_____

**4.** How do you think trade with the Europeans helped to finance building programs within Safavid Persia?

_____

_____

## Critical Thinking: Movement

What negative effect might the exporting of precious jewels and gold have had on the Mughal Empire?

_____

_____

_____

_____

Copyright © by Holt, Rinehart and Winston. All rights reserved.

# Geography Activity

Modern Chapter **10**

## Monarchs of Europe

### THE THIRTY YEARS' WAR

The Thirty Years' War was sparked by years of struggle over religious beliefs. Beginning in Prague in 1618, the war quickly spread throughout Germany. The conflict expanded to include national interests. Catholic France sided with Protestant forces in order to counteract the might of the Habsburg family. By the time the war ended with the Treaty of Westphalia in 1648, approximately one third of the German population had died. Territorial changes were fairly minor. However, the treaty did affirm a ruler's right to choose the religion of his or her territory. Study the map below and answer the questions that follow.

### The Treaty of Westphalia, 1648

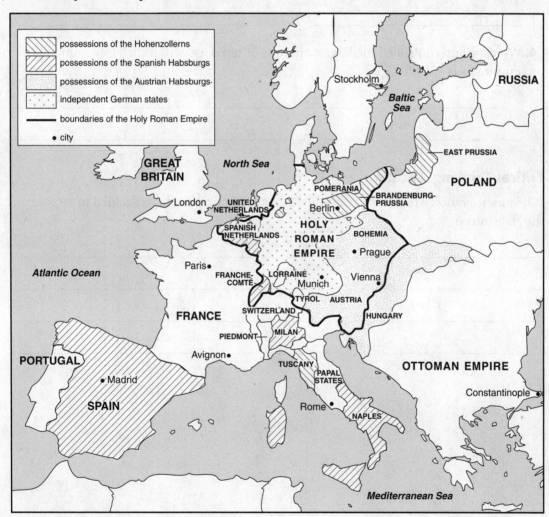

**Chapter 19, Geography Activity, continued**

**1.** What territories were controlled by the Spanish Habsburgs?

_____

_____

**2.** What territories were controlled by the Hohenzollerns?

_____

_____

**3.** What group controlled Prague and the surrounding area?

_____

_____

**4.** Which group controlled the largest amount of territory within the Holy Roman Empire in 1648?

_____

_____

## Critical Thinking: Location

Why might France, which controlled the province of Lorraine, have decided to oppose the Habsburgs?

_____

_____

_____

_____

Copyright © by Holt, Rinehart and Winston. All rights reserved.

# CHAPTER 20

Modern Chapter 11

## Geography Activity

# Enlightenment and Revolution in England and America

## THE SETTLING OF THE ENGLISH COLONIES

Between 1641 and 1760 the population of the English colonies on the North American mainland rose from 50,000 to approximately 1.6 million, expanding into new territory as it grew. The map below shows the spread of English colonial settlement during this period. Examine the map, and answer the questions that follow.

## Colonial Settlement

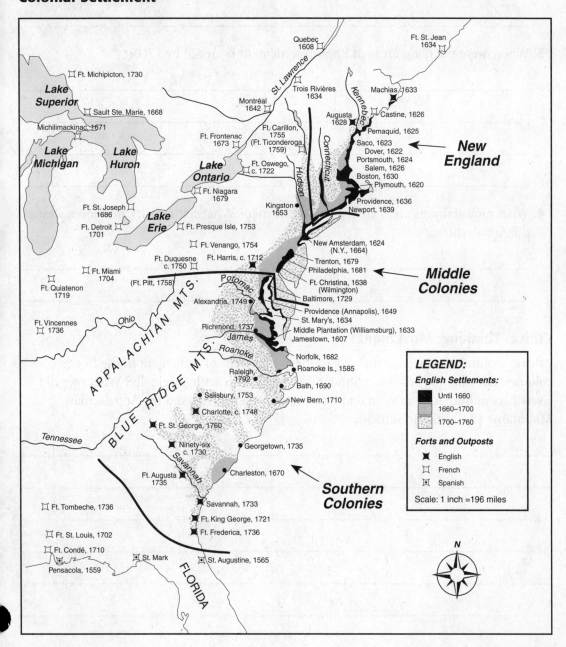

Copyright © by Holt, Rinehart and Winston. All rights reserved.

**Chapter 20, Geography Activity, continued**

1. What three English colonial regions are shown on the map?

_____

_____

2. What were the names and founding dates of the earliest English, French, and Spanish settlements shown on this map? What geographic characteristics did these settlements have in common?

_____

_____

3. Where were the main areas of English settlement by 1660? by 1760?

_____

_____

_____

_____

4. What mountainous areas are shown on the map? What settlements are shown west of the Appalachians?

_____

_____

## Critical Thinking: Movement

After examining the map carefully, describe the patterns of settlement in the English colonies. On what part of the continent did the English settle originally? What role did rivers play in human migration and town development? How did the Appalachian Mountains affect English settlement?

_____

_____

_____

_____

_____

Copyright © by Holt, Rinehart and Winston. All rights reserved.

# CHAPTER **21**

Geography Activity

Modern Chapter **12**    **The French Revolution and Napoléon**

## NAPOLÉON'S DISASTROUS RUSSIAN CAMPAIGN

One historian summed up Napoléon's military campaign in Russia in 1812 with these words: "The problems of space, time, and distance proved too great for even one of the greatest military minds that ever existed." Napoléon made several serious mistakes. First, he never expected that he would travel all the way to Moscow. He was used to defeating an enemy after only one or two battles. After its defeat, the enemy would ask for peace. Napoléon expected to defeat the Russians far short of Moscow.

He also gravely miscalculated the problems of feeding, equipping, and moving several hundred thousand troops in Russia. The roads were terrible. Supplies often were delayed weeks or even months. The Russians destroyed their own grain and livestock to keep supplies from the French.

Two months after starting out, French supply lines were overextended and the size of the army had been reduced by fighting along the way. At this point, Napoléon made a critical decision. Because the Russians would not fight a major battle, he would simply press on. He would capture Moscow and bring them to their knees. The Russians gave Napoléon his long-awaited fight 70 miles west of Moscow, on the field of Borodino. It was a bloodbath for both sides, but it was indecisive. One week later, Napoléon entered Moscow.

Napoléon expected the Russians to ask for peace terms, but they did not. Moreover, the Russians had destroyed Moscow as they withdrew. As a result, the French troops could not find housing. The Russians hoped that Napoléon would be defeated by the bitter cold of the Russian winter. The first frost and snow were only two weeks away when Napoléon decided to lead his army back to France.

## Temperature and Troop Losses

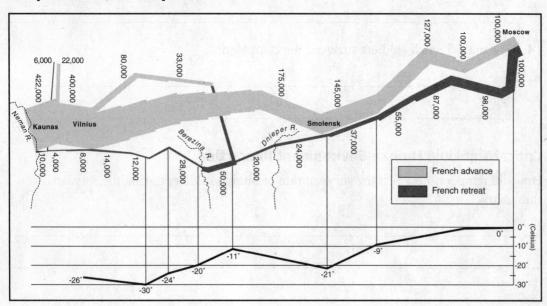

Chapter 21, Geography Activity, continued

On October 24 the Russians attacked the retreating French as they tried to cross the Lusha River at Maloyaroslavets. The French won the battle, but at a cost of seven generals and 4,000 men. By November 25 the French had reached the Berezina River near Borisov. Here the Russians had knocked down the bridges and fortified the river banks. Napoléon's forces quickly built two new bridges. But in their panic to cross, thousands died in the freezing waters.

The chart illustrates French losses during the Russian campaign. At the left, the thick band shows the size of the army as it invaded Russia. The width of the band shows the size of the army at each position. Napoléon's retreat from Russia is shown by the dark lower band. Examine the chart, and answer the questions that follow.

**1.** What natural barriers did the French have to cross in their journey? How did the Russians make use of these barriers?

_____

_____

_____

**2.** According to the chart, how many French soldiers began the Russian campaign?

_____

**3.** What was the temperature when the French army reached Smolensk during their retreat?

_____

_____

**4.** How many French soldiers survived the campaign?

_____

_____

## Critical Thinking: Human-Environment Interaction

How did temperature affect the survival rate of French soldiers during the Russian campaign?

_____

_____

_____

Copyright © by Holt, Rinehart and Winston. All rights reserved.

Name _____ Class _____ Date _____

Modern Chapter **13**                                    **The Industrial Revolution**

## MANCHESTER: THE GROWTH OF AN INDUSTRIAL GIANT

The city of Manchester in northwestern England began as a Roman fort about A.D. 70 or 80. A little more than 600 years later, Anglo-Saxons from northeastern England founded a village on the site, where three rivers meet. Over the years the village grew into a busy trading center. In 1227 it was granted a charter by the king to run an annual trade fair. Nestled in an area good for growing flax and raising sheep, by the 1600s Manchester had become a center for producing, finishing, and selling textiles such as linen and wool. During that same century, imported raw cotton further expanded the city's important textile industry.

During the 1700s the population of Manchester grew rapidly. This was partly the result of the enclosure movement, which forced many small landowners to sell their farms and move to the cities. Manchester, which had had a population of 16,000 in 1750, grew to 25,000 by 1772 and to 70,000 by 1800. The city's rapid growth in population in the late 1700s mainly resulted from the Industrial Revolution.

Steam power was first applied to the spinning of cotton in Manchester in 1789. Only six years later, the production of cotton was the city's chief economic activity. Manchester had become the center of England's cotton production.

The Industrial Revolution was turning Manchester into an industrial giant. Within 50 years, the city's population would approach half a million people. Study the map below and answer the questions that follow.

## Industrial Development in Manchester

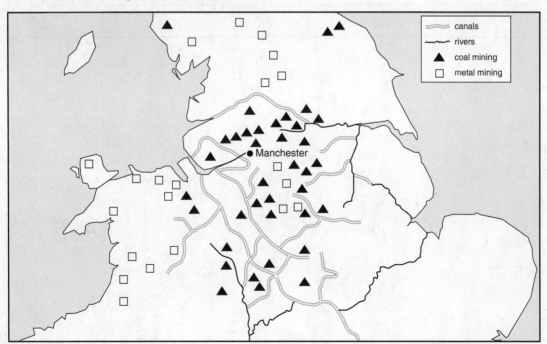

Copyright © by Holt, Rinehart and Winston. All rights reserved.

**Chapter 22, Geography Activity, continued**

**1.** What raw materials were available in the area around Manchester?

_____

_____

**2.** How did transportation aid in the development of Manchester as an industrial city?

_____

_____

**3.** How did geography affect Manchester's industrial development?

_____

_____

## Critical Thinking: Movement

How did changes in agriculture contribute to the development of industry in Manchester?

_____

_____

_____

_____

Copyright © by Holt, Rinehart and Winston. All rights reserved.

Name _____ Class _____ Date _____

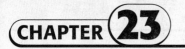
## NEW YORK: THE NEW INDUSTRIAL CITY

By 1900 some two million Russian, Irish, German, and Italian immigrants lived in New York City. These immigrants often clustered together by nationality, creating a patchwork quilt of ethnic neighborhoods across the city. The map below shows this pattern in the borough of Manhattan in 1910. Floor plans of a row of typical New York City tenement buildings also are shown. Examine the map and diagram below and answer the questions that follow.

## Immigrant Origins of Manhattan Residents, 1910

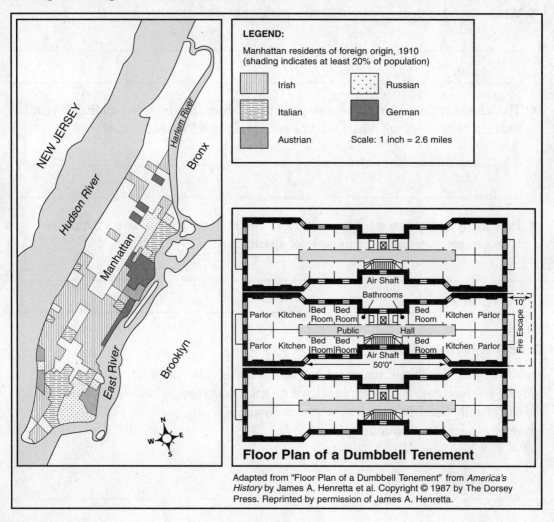

**LEGEND:**

Manhattan residents of foreign origin, 1910
(shading indicates at least 20% of population)

Irish

Italian

Austrian

Russian

German

Scale: 1 inch = 2.6 miles

**Floor Plan of a Dumbbell Tenement**

Adapted from "Floor Plan of a Dumbbell Tenement" from *America's History* by James A. Henretta et al. Copyright © 1987 by The Dorsey Press. Reprinted by permission of James A. Henretta.

Copyright © by Holt, Rinehart and Winston. All rights reserved.

**Chapter 23, Geography Activity, continued**

**1.** What boroughs of New York City are labeled on the map? What state is labeled?

_____

_____

**2.** How long and wide is Manhattan? What national groups are shown there in 1910? What was the predominant immigrant group in Manhattan?

_____

_____

**3.** Where were Manhattan's non-immigrant neighborhoods concentrated?

_____

_____

**4.** The tenement floor plan shows a single floor of three side-by-side buildings. What lay between each building? Where was the emergency exit located?

_____

_____

**5.** How many bathrooms were on each floor? Did each apartment have a bathroom? How can you determine the number of apartments?

_____

_____

## Critical Thinking: Place

Each floor of a "dumbbell" tenement, the kind shown on the diagram, was just 25 feet wide by 100 feet long. If four families lived on each floor, approximately how much space did each family have? What would be the drawback of living in such a place? What advantages might the community offer?

_____

_____

_____

_____

_____

Copyright © by Holt, Rinehart and Winston. All rights reserved.

## CHAPTER 24    Geography Activity

Modern Chapter 15    **The Age of Reform**

### THE SLAVE TRADE IN THE UNITED STATES

By the mid-1800s the internal slave trade was flourishing in the southern United States. Two factors fueled this trade: the abolition of the African slave trade in 1808 and the westward expansion of plantation agriculture. As a result, thousands of enslaved African Americans were forcibly removed to new plantations on the southern frontier. The map below shows the main slave trade routes and principal agricultural regions of the South in 1860. Examine the map, and answer the questions that follow.

### Southern Agriculture and the Slave Trade, 1860

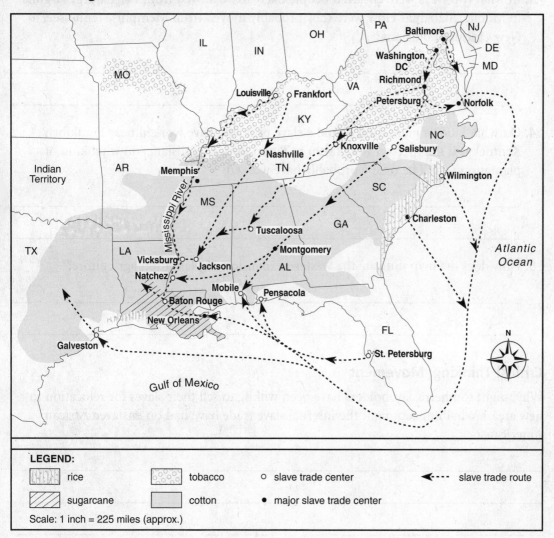

Copyright © by Holt, Rinehart and Winston. All rights reserved.

**1.** What crops are shown on the map? Where was rice grown?

_____

_____

**2.** What major slave trade centers are shown? What slave trade center was in Texas?

_____

_____

**3.** In what two ways were enslaved people likely to be moved from Petersburg, Virginia, to Mobile, Alabama? How were they probably moved from Memphis, Tennessee, to New Orleans, Louisiana?

_____

_____

**4.** On what kind of plantation would a slave probably have worked near Frankfort, Kentucky? If that person were taken to Baton Rouge, Louisiana, on what kind of plantation would he or she probably have worked?

_____

_____

**5.** How does the map indicate the western expansion of plantation agriculture?

_____

_____

## Critical Thinking: Movement

Why might southern slaveholders have been willing to sell their slaves for relocation to new areas? What impact might the internal slave trade have had on enslaved African Americans?

_____

_____

_____

_____

_____

Copyright © by Holt, Rinehart and Winston. All rights reserved.

# CHAPTER 25

Modern Chapter **16**

## Geography Activity

## Nationalism in Europe

### CONNECTING EASTERN AND WESTERN RUSSIA

In 1891 the Russian government began a huge project—constructing a railroad from western Russia across Siberia to Vladivostok, a Pacific Ocean port. This Trans-Siberian Railroad was initiated by Count S. Y. Witte. Russia's minister of finance, Witte also was a railroad engineer. He expected the railroad to open "a new avenue and new horizons to world commerce."

Witte believed that Russia could become self-sufficient by making fuller use of its own natural resources and by expanding the area of settlement within its borders. He also hoped to expand the Russian economy, in large part by increasing trade.

Witte considered Siberia a major element in this policy. Siberia itself covers one half of Russia's land area, or 5 million square miles. Yet in the 1800s its resources barely had been touched. This was due in large part to Siberia's severe climate, with winter temperatures that plunge to -90° F. In the early 1800s only about 500,000 people lived there. During that century, however, a major migration took place from Russia's overpopulated rural areas to Siberia. Witte wanted this migration not only to continue but also to increase.

Witte's policy called for more Siberian land to be used for grain growing and livestock raising to help feed Russia's people. He also saw Siberia as a provider of natural resources for Russia's industrial development. For years silver, gold, copper, and lead had been mined in Siberia. It was also well known that Siberia had coal reserves as well as millions of trees for lumbering.

Witte's device for opening up Siberia was the Trans-Siberian Railroad. As years passed, more natural resources were found in Siberia, including plentiful reserves of coal. Great deposits of oil, natural gas, diamonds, platinum, tin, and tungsten were abundant as well. The railroad made it possible to ship these resources to the heavily populated eastern portion of Russia and to Russia's Pacific port of Vladivostok. The railroad also contributed to the development of cities along its route, thus expanding Russian settlement in Siberia. Study the map below and answer the questions that follow.

### The Trans-Siberian Railroad

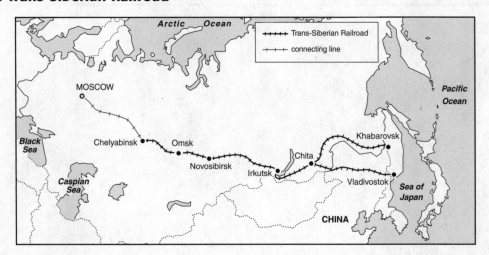

Copyright © by Holt, Rinehart and Winston. All rights reserved.

## Chapter 25, Geography Activity, continued

**1.** What was the westernmost point of the Trans-Siberian railroad?

_____

_____

**2.** What city was linked to the railroad by a connecting line?

_____

_____

**3.** Through what towns did the railroad pass?

_____

_____

**4.** Through what other country did the railroad pass?

_____

_____

## Critical Thinking: Movement

How did the Trans-Siberian Railroad contribute to Russia's industrialization and commerce?

_____

_____

_____

_____

Copyright © by Holt, Rinehart and Winston. All rights reserved.

# CHAPTER 26

Modern Chapter 17

## Geography Activity

## The Age of Imperialism

## MIGRATION PATTERNS IN SOUTHERN AFRICA

Patterns of settlement in Africa were constantly in transition after the Europeans arrived. Studying the geography of the region allows us to see how political changes affected the average person. Clashes were common in this region during this period. The British were at odds with the Boers. The Zulus were fighting the Europeans as well as other Africans. All of these conflicts led to migrations by several groups throughout this region. Study the map below and answer the questions that follow.

## European and African Migration, 1800s

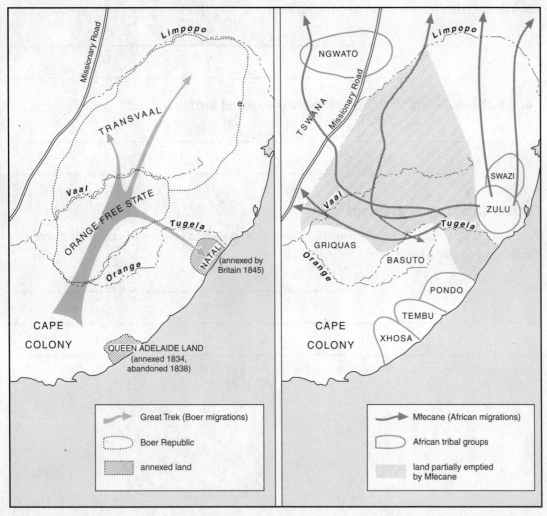

Adaptation of "White Migrations" and "Black Migrations" from *Africa Since 1800* by Roland Oliver and Anthony Atmore. Copyright © 1972 by **Columbia University Press.** Reprinted by permission of the publisher.

Copyright © by Holt, Rinehart and Winston. All rights reserved.

**Chapter 26, Geography Activity, continued**

1. In relation to the Cape Colony, which direction did the Great Trek follow?

_____

_____

2. In relation to the land left partially emptied by *mfecane*, in which direction was African migration taking place?

_____

_____

3. What territories were annexed by the British?

_____

_____

4. Which group—the Africans or the Boers—moved further inland?

_____

_____

## Critical Thinking: Movement

Based upon this map, what do you think would be possible sources of conflict between the Boers and the Africans?

_____

_____

_____

Copyright © by Holt, Rinehart and Winston. All rights reserved.

# CHAPTER 27

Geography Activity

Modern Chapter 18     **World War I and the Russian Revolution**

## WORLD WAR I

The countries that took part in World War I committed millions of troops to the fighting and suffered heavy casualties. The map below provides information on the numbers of troops contributed by the various nations fighting on both sides of the war. Examine the map, and answer the questions that follow.

## Troop Strength

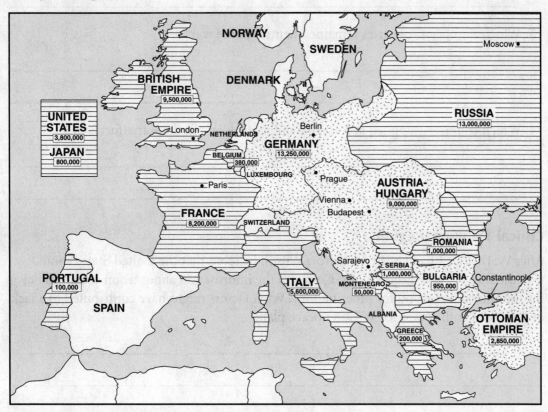

**LEGEND:**

| | | | |
|---|---|---|---|
| ▨ | Central Powers, 1917 | 50,000 | total mobilized forces |
| ▤ | Allied Powers, 1917 | • | major cities |
| ☐ | neutral countries | Scale: 1 inch = 325 miles (approx.) | |

Copyright © by Holt, Rinehart and Winston. All rights reserved.

**Chapter 27, Geography Activity, continued**

**1.** Which countries belonged to the Allied Powers?

_____

**2.** Which countries belonged to the Central Powers?

_____

_____

**3.** Which European countries remained neutral in the war?

_____

_____

**4.** Which countries supplied at least one million soldiers to the war effort?

_____

_____

## Critical Thinking: Region

After World War I had ended, Woodrow Wilson believed that the United States should take the lead in peace negotiations. Compare the information about troop commitment for the United States and for other nations. What factors might have contributed to a lack of European enthusiasm for Wilson's peace plan?

_____

_____

_____

_____

_____

Copyright © by Holt, Rinehart and Winston. All rights reserved.

# CHAPTER 28

Modern Chapter **19**

Geography Activity

## The Great Depression and the Rise of Totalitarianism

### THE FAILURE OF WORLD REVOLUTION, 1917–1927

Many Bolsheviks hoped that their success in Russia would lead to a rapid seizure of power by communists throughout Europe. In 1919 the Russian Communists established the Comintern, or Communist International. This group united all the Communist parties of the world in a revolutionary organization. Communist uprisings in several places succeeded temporarily—for five months in Hungary and for several weeks in both Slovakia and Bavaria. Overall the Comintern's attempts to promote revolution in other countries ultimately failed. No communist regime other than the Soviet Union successfully came to power anywhere in Europe in the decade following the Russian Revolution. Study the map below, and answer the questions that follow.

### Communism and Revolution

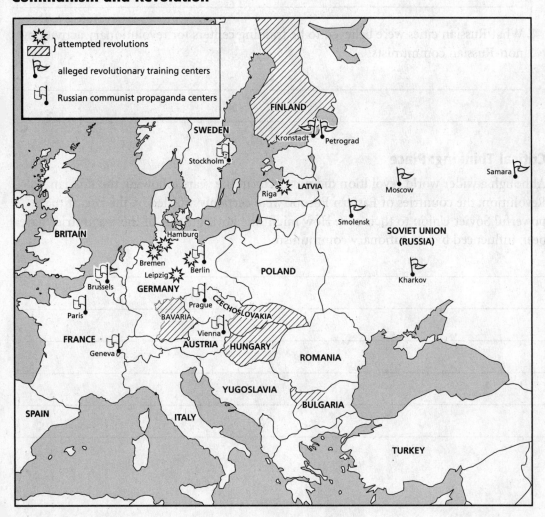

Copyright © by Holt, Rinehart and Winston. All rights reserved.

**Chapter 28, Geography Activity, continued**

**1.** In what countries did communists make revolutionary attempts to seize power in the decade following the Russian Revolution?

_____

_____

**2.** In what cities did communists attempt to seize power during this period?

_____

_____

**3.** What cities outside Russia were Russian communist propaganda centers?

_____

_____

**4.** What Russian cities were believed to be training centers for revolutionary activity by non-Russian communists?

_____

_____

## Critical Thinking: Place

Although a wider world revolution did not occur in the years following the Russian Revolution, the countries of Eastern Europe were certainly affected by the rise of the powerful Soviet Union to their east. How might the governments of these countries have been influenced by revolutionary communism?

_____

_____

_____

_____

_____

Copyright © by Holt, Rinehart and Winston. All rights reserved.

# CHAPTER 29

Geography Activity

Modern Chapter 20 **Nationalist Movements Around the World**

## THE PHILIPPINE WAR

Maps allow us to visualize historical events. Maps are particularly crucial in describing the events that took place in a war. In the late 1800s, the people of the Philippines had struggled for independence against the Spanish. In this effort, local nationalists enlisted the help of the United States. After the war, the United States wanted to control the Philippines. Filipinos resisted the presence of the Americans just as they had resisted the presence of the Spanish. By 1935, the Philippines had achieved full self-government, with the promise of complete independence in 10 years. Using the map below, answer the following questions.

## Philippines

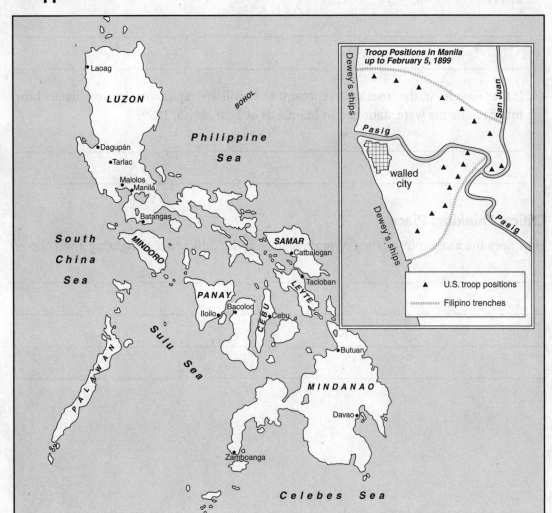

Copyright © by Holt, Rinehart and Winston. All rights reserved.

Chapter 29, Geography Activity, continued

**1.** What major Philippine city was the site of much troop activity?

_____

_____

**2.** What impact did Manila's coastal location have on a possible military strategy for the United States?

_____

_____

_____

**3.** How did the construction of trenches relate to the location of the San Juan and Pasig Rivers?

_____

_____

_____

**4.** If the triangles in the inset map represent U.S. military regiments, approximately how many regiments were stationed in Manila as of February 5, 1899?

_____

_____

## Critical Thinking: Place

How does the geography of the Philippines suggest the difficulties of fighting a war there?

_____

_____

_____

_____

Copyright © by Holt, Rinehart and Winston. All rights reserved.

Name _____ Class _____ Date _____

## JAPAN'S DRIVE TO EXPAND IN MANCHURIA

The island nation of Japan had long wanted to expand into Manchuria, the northeastern region of China. "Manchuria is for the Japanese the only region for expansion. . . . As Asians, the Japanese must of necessity live in Asia." These were the words of Japanese military leader Yamagato Aritomo early in the 1900s.

Why were the Japanese so eager for expansion? The table below gives some clues. The rate of natural increase of Japan's population was 12.8 per 1,000 each year. The vast area of Manchuria offered plenty of room for Japanese migration. It also had the advantage of lying fairly close to the Japanese homeland. Manchuria also had the natural resources that Japan lacked. Manchuria also could supply the food that Japan needed to import in great quantity.

The Russians, too, wanted to control Manchuria. This conflict led to the Russo-Japanese War in 1904. When the war ended in 1905, Japan regained control of southern Manchuria. Japan began its expansion there, building railroads and plants to manufacture iron and steel. By the 1920s about one million Japanese had moved to Manchuria. The Chinese then began trying to reestablish control in Manchuria. They built railroad lines to compete with the Japanese lines. Japanese military leaders feared that these actions would threaten their interests in Manchuria. They therefore set the stage to take over all of Manchuria.

On September 18, 1931, the Japanese blew up a section of its own Southern Manchurian Railway at Mukden. They claimed that the act had been committed by the Chinese. Within 24 hours Japanese troops had captured all the key cities along the railroad. Soon the Japanese had conquered all of Manchuria.

The League of Nations and the United States condemned this Japanese aggression. In response, Japan withdrew from the international organization. The Japanese then increased their agricultural and industrial buildup in Manchuria.

## Japan and Manchuria in the Early 1900s

|  | Japan | Manchuria |
|---|---|---|
| Land Area | 144,000 square miles | 475,000 square miles |
| Population | 49 million | 14 million |
| Fertile Soil | 15% of the land usable for farming | large area containing some of the best farmland in China |
| Iron Ore | almost none | rich deposits |
| Coal | a good supply, but unsuitable for many industrial purposes | rich deposits of industrial quality |
| Petroleum | almost none | rich deposits |

Copyright © by Holt, Rinehart and Winston. All rights reserved.

Name _____  Class _____  Date _____

**Chapter 30, Geography Activity, continued**

**1.** How did the population of Japan compare to the population of Manchuria? How did the land areas of the two regions compare?

_____

_____

**2.** Approximately how many square miles of land in Japan were usable for farming?

_____

_____

**3.** Why did so much food need to be imported to Japan?

_____

_____

**4.** How did natural resources in Manchuria enable the Japanese to make the region an important supply base?

_____

_____

## Critical Thinking: Human-Environment Interaction

How might the natural resources listed in the chart have contributed to Japanese industrial development in Manchuria?

_____

_____

_____

_____

_____

_____

Copyright © by Holt, Rinehart and Winston. All rights reserved.

Modern Chapter **22**

**Europe and North America
in the Postwar Years**

## THE BERLIN WALL

At the end of World War II, the Allied powers divided Berlin into four sectors. The French, British, and American sectors were known as West Berlin. The Soviet sector was known as East Berlin. In August 1961, Soviet and East German troops and police began to construct a huge wall separating East and West Berlin. The map below shows the different sectors of Berlin. Examine the map, and answer the questions that follow.

## The Berlin Wall

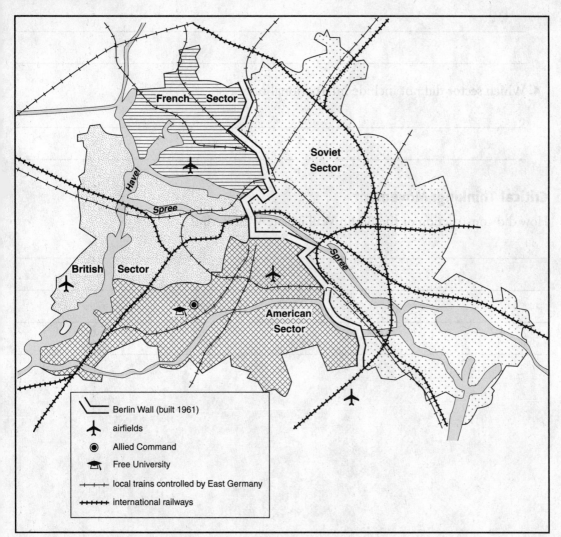

Chapter 31, Geography Activity, continued

1. Which sector contained the Allied Command?

_____

_____

2. What airports appear on the map, and in which sectors were they located?

_____

_____

3. Where was the Free University?

_____

_____

4. Which sector did not include international railways?

_____

_____

## Critical Thinking: Movement

How did construction of the Berlin Wall isolate West Berlin?

_____

_____

_____

_____

Copyright © by Holt, Rinehart and Winston. All rights reserved.

# CHAPTER 32 Geography Activity

## Modern Chapter 23

### Asia Since 1945

## AGRICULTURE IN CHINA

China's greatest agricultural development has taken place in the eastern part of the country, where rivers and rich soil have made farms productive. The map below shows the organization of Chinese agriculture in 1966, the year the Cultural Revolution began. Examine the map below, and answer the questions that follow.

## Crop Production in China

Major crop regions:
1 Northeast: soybean, spring wheat, kaoliang
2 Northwest: spring wheat, millet
3 Loess plateau: winter wheat, millet
4 North China: winter wheat, kaoliang
5 Ssu-ch'uan: rice, sweet potato, field peas
6 Yangzi: winter wheat, rice
7 Southwest plateau: rice
8 Southeast: rice, tea, tung
9 Lingnan: double-crop rice

at least 60% of land under cultivation

Copyright © by Holt, Rinehart and Winston. All rights reserved.

Chapter 32, Geography Activity, continued

**1.** In what crop regions were spring wheat, winter wheat, rice, or double-crop rice grown?

_____

_____

_____

**2.** Which crop region included Hainan?

_____

_____

**3.** Which crop region produced tea?

_____

_____

**4.** What crops were grown in region 5?

_____

_____

**5.** Which crop region did not include areas in which at least 60 percent of the land was under cultivation?

_____

_____

## Critical Thinking: Human-Environment Interaction

In 1966 the areas of greatest industrial development overlapped with crop regions 1, 2, 3, 4, and 6. How might industrial development have affected agricultural development?

_____

_____

_____

Copyright © by Holt, Rinehart and Winston. All rights reserved.

# CHAPTER 33

## Geography Activity

Modern Chapter 24    **Africa and the Middle East Since 1945**

### POPULATION IN MODERN AFRICA

Africa's geography is extremely varied, from deserts to rainforests. Geography often plays an important role in the establishment and development of population centers. The map below shows population density throughout Africa in 1990. Study the map and answer the questions that follow.

## Population Distribution in Africa

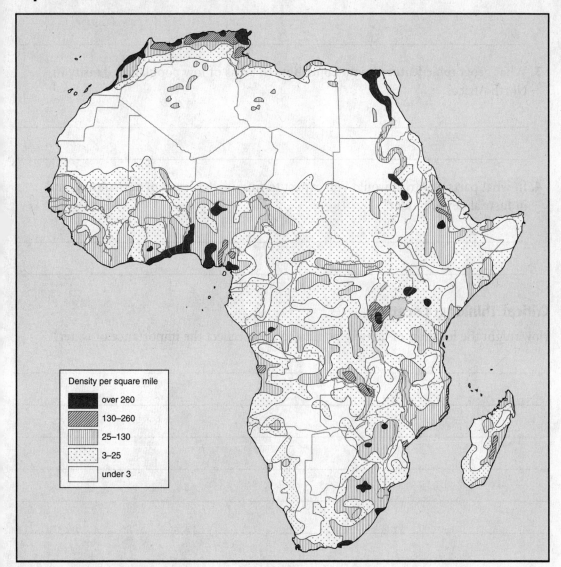

Density per square mile

- over 260
- 130–260
- 25–130
- 3–25
- under 3

Copyright © by Holt, Rinehart and Winston. All rights reserved.

Name _____ Class _____ Date _____

**Chapter 33, Geography Activity, continued**

**1.** What regions of Africa have the greatest number of areas with more than 260 people per square mile?

_____

_____

**2.** Do most areas with more than 260 people per square mile lie in northern or southern Africa?

_____

_____

**3.** What geographic feature might contribute to areas of low population density in North Africa?

_____

_____

**4.** In what parts of Africa would you expect to find higher levels of agricultural and industrial development?

_____

_____

## Critical Thinking: Location

How might the location of densely populated areas reflect the importance of water?

_____

_____

_____

_____

_____

Copyright © by Holt, Rinehart and Winston. All rights reserved.

## CHAPTER **34**

Modern Chapter **25**

Geography Activity

**Latin America Since 1945**

### NEW DIRECTIONS IN LATIN AMERICA

Many efforts have been made to strengthen the economies of Latin American nations through industrial development. Perhaps the boldest effort is currently being made in the northern Amazon rain forest of Brazil. There, a massive land-use experiment is underway in an area the size of Connecticut. On land lying along the Jari River, a tributary of the Amazon, a giant paper-pulp industry is emerging. It is the brainchild of American billionaire Daniel K. Ludwig, who began the project in 1967.

The Amazon experiment is an attempt to make use of the natural assets of the area—its climate and soil. Ludwig's plan included converting dense rain forest into a giant plantation of fast-growing trees. He believed such trees could then provide a continuing source of wood that could be harvested and processed. The fast-growing trees could supply three times as much wood in one year as the slow-growing natural trees could. This would help meet the world's growing demand for wood and paper.

The first step in the project was to begin cutting down the natural forest, harvesting the wood with sales value, and burning the valueless wood. Next, seemingly endless rows of fast-growing trees—Caribbean pine and eucalyptus—were planted. By the late 1970s thousands of them were ready to be harvested.

To make it possible to process them on the Jari site, Ludwig took a daring step. He hired a Japanese firm to build a paper-pulp factory and a power plant in Japan. Each plant was 20 stories high, and as long as two and one half football fields. When the plants were finished, Ludwig had them floated 15,500 miles from Japan to the Brazilian coast and up the Amazon to the Jari.

The cost of building and shipping the plants was a staggering $269 million. This was still less expensive than trying to assemble the plants from scratch in the rain forest. Ludwig estimated that he was spending $180,000 a day on the project. By 1980 the total cost of the project had reached $1 billion.

By that time, the Jari manager reported that the pulp factory was producing about 750 tons of pulp a day: "That's worth more than $300,000 each day—enough to cover the cost of felling [cutting down] native forest, planting pulp trees, and providing for the 30,000 people [the workers and their families] who already live off this operation." In the long run, though, can something that cost so much to develop and to run be truly profitable? That question remains to be answered. In 1982 Ludwig seemed to be facing some economic difficulties of his own. He sold his Jari holdings to a group of Brazilian investors.

In addition to the question of whether it can ever be profitable, the project raises questions of ecology. Some environmentalists worry that the rain forest soil is too fragile to produce stands of trees continuously. Others wonder if cutting down the native forest will lead to soil erosion. The erosion, in turn, would cause silt to clog the streams and possibly change the direction of their flow. Some scientists fear that removing

**Jari Forestry Project**

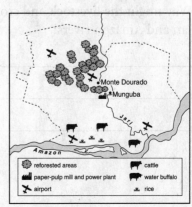

reforested areas      cattle
paper-pulp mill and power plant      water buffalo
airport      rice

Copyright © by Holt, Rinehart and Winston. All rights reserved.

Chapter 34, Geography Activity, continued

the natural forest will cause a change in climate. Study the map on page 67, and answer the questions that follow.

**1.** Near what town are the paper-pulp factory and power plant located?

_____

_____

**2.** What town is closest to an airport?

_____

_____

**3.** What reason might Ludwig have had for building the towns downriver from most of the reforested areas?

_____

_____

_____

_____

**4.** Part of Ludwig's plan involved producing food both for the people living on the Jari site and for export. What evidence do you find that this plan is being carried out?

_____

_____

_____

_____

## Critical Thinking: Location

Why might the livestock and crop-production areas be located near the junction of the Jari and Amazon rivers?

_____

_____

_____

Copyright © by Holt, Rinehart and Winston. All rights reserved.

## CHAPTER 35

Modern Chapter 26

Geography Activity

## The Superpowers in the Modern Era

### AFTER THE COLD WAR

The United States-Soviet Union relations greatly changed during Richard Nixon's presidency. Tensions were released by the signing of the Strategic Arms Limitations Treaty (SALT) in 1972, which acted to decrease the likelihood of nuclear war. President Jimmy Carter continued this policy during his presidency, instituting his policy of *détente*, which means "easing of strain."

This period ended during Ronald Reagan's presidency when the Soviet Union invaded Afghanistan in 1979. During this time Reagan increased military spending and updated the United States' nuclear arsenal. However, in the early 1990s both superpowers agreed

## Breakup of the Soviet Sphere

Copyright © by Holt, Rinehart and Winston. All rights reserved.

Chapter 35, Geography Activity, continued

to eliminate some nuclear weapons and the Soviet Union reduced its military pressure in Afghanistan.

Challenges to the communist stronghold began to unravel the Soviet Union by the late 1980s. Smaller communist nations broke away from the Soviet Union and declared their independence. This ultimately led to the unraveling of the Soviet Union. At the same time, Europe began to come together financially to gain strength and to obtain a place among the superpowers. Europe realized that by having separate financial systems in each of its countries, it could not command the power that larger powers did. This led to the formation of the European Union in 1993. This Union offered economic stability to this region. Study the map on the previous page, and answer the questions that follow.

**1.** Why might the European Union make Europe a major player in the world market?

_____

_____

**2.** Why would the United States and the Soviet Union have wanted to control each other's use of nuclear arms?

_____

_____

**3.** Why would financial strength along with nuclear capacity automatically make a country a superpower?

_____

_____

**4.** President Nixon sought to relieve tensions between the United States and the Soviet Union by decreasing nuclear capacity. Why was nuclear war so important to control?

_____

_____

## Critical Thinking: Human-Environment Interaction

How do you think SALT might have added to the rebellion by former Soviet communist countries? Would the decrease of nuclear arms have made them feel as if it was safer to rebel against Soviet Union control? Why or why not?

_____

_____

Copyright © by Holt, Rinehart and Winston. All rights reserved.

# CHAPTER 36

Modern Chapter **27**

Geography Activity

## The Modern World

## THE EXPANDING SAHARA

The expanding Sahara is among Africa's most serious problems. Already the size of the continental United States, the desert continues to grow. Each year, the nations whose territory includes the Sahara lose precious farming and grazing land to the expanding desert. This loss results in a decrease in the earning ability of the population.

It may seem difficult to imagine today, but 2,500 years ago vast areas of this dry wasteland were teeming with plant and animal life. The Greek historian Herodotus described forests and wildlife and cereal-producing fields in areas now part of the Sahara. A more recent writer reported that the Sahara was once a prosperous part of the Roman Empire.

What led to such a drastic and far-reaching change? In part, the answer is climate. There has been some lessening in rainfall over the past 2,000 years. A larger part of the answer may lie in use of the land in a way that eventually leads to changes in the environment. It began when the Romans cut down vast forests for building materials and fuel. They made no effort to replant the trees. In time, the stripped topsoil was washed away by rain and blown away by wind. As the topsoil was lost, crops diminished. Instead of farming the land, people used it to graze their sheep and goats. Through overgrazing, the soil finally dried up and grew nothing. Farming and grazing land became desert.

The process continued through the centuries and goes on today. Subsistence farmers and herders live on the lands that ring the desert. In years of good rainfall, they traditionally use as much of this land as possible for grazing and for growing wheat and barley. This has at least two effects on the land. First, because the amount of grazing land is lessened, that which remains is overgrazed by the herds. The overuse kills off vegetation for good and leads to soil erosion. Second, by tradition, the farmers harvest barley by pulling it out of the ground, roots and all. (The roots make good animal feed.) This method of harvesting loosens the soil and exposes it to wind erosion.

## Land Use and the Sahara

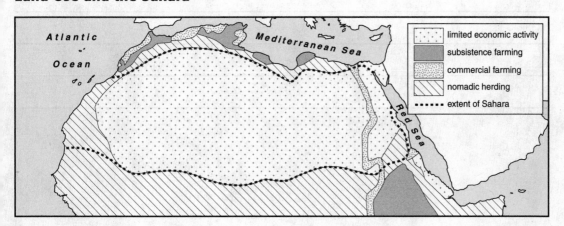

Chapter 36, Geography Activity, continued

**1.** How has land use in the Sahara changed over the past several thousand years?

_____

_____

_____

_____

**2.** What major types of land use take place within the Sahara?

_____

_____

_____

**3.** What traditions have played a role in causing the Sahara to expand?

_____

_____

_____

**4.** How does the expansion of the Sahara affect agriculture?

_____

_____

_____

## Critical Thinking: Human-Environment Interaction

How might the spread of the Sahara be encouraged by the types of land use shown on the map?

_____

_____

_____

_____

Copyright © by Holt, Rinehart and Winston. All rights reserved.

Geography Activity

## The Modern World

### AFTER THE COLD WAR

The United States-Soviet Union relations greatly changed during Richard Nixon's presidency. Tensions were released by the signing of the Strategic Arms Limitations Treaty (SALT) in 1972, which acted to decrease the likelihood of nuclear war. President Jimmy Carter continued this policy during his presidency, instituting his policy of *détente*, which means "easing of strain."

This period ended during Ronald Reagan's presidency when the Soviet Union invaded Afghanistan in 1979. During this time Reagan increased military spending and updated the United States' nuclear arsenal. However, in the early 1990s both superpowers agreed

## Breakup of the Soviet Sphere

## Epilogue, Geography Activity, continued

to eliminate some nuclear weapons and the Soviet Union reduced its military pressure in Afghanistan.

Challenges to the communist stronghold began to unravel the Soviet Union by the late 1980s. Smaller communist nations broke away from the Soviet Union and declared their independence. This ultimately led to the unraveling of the Soviet Union. At the same time, Europe began to come together financially to gain strength and to obtain a place among the superpowers. Europe realized that by having separate financial systems in each of its countries, it could not command the power that larger powers did. This led to the formation of the European Union in 1993. This Union offered economic stability to this region. Study the map on the previous page, and answer the questions that follow.

**1.** Why might the European Union make Europe a major player in the world market?

_____

_____

**2.** Why would the United States and the Soviet Union have wanted to control each other's use of nuclear arms?

_____

_____

**3.** Why would financial strength along with nuclear capacity automatically make a country a superpower?

_____

_____

**4.** President Nixon sought to relieve tensions between the United States and the Soviet Union by decreasing nuclear capacity. Why was nuclear war so important to control?

_____

_____

## Critical Thinking: Human-Environment Interaction

How do you think SALT might have added to the rebellion by former Soviet communist countries? Would the decrease of nuclear arms have made them feel as if it was safer to rebel against Soviet Union control? Why or why not?

_____

_____

Copyright © by Holt, Rinehart and Winston. All rights reserved.

## PROLOGUE


# Geography Activity
## The Ancient World

## THE SPREAD OF IRONWORKING

Geographical isolation, climate differences, and geographic diversity were three critical factors in shaping the cultures of the vast continent of Africa. In East Africa, settlers spread down the Rift Valley from Ethiopia. Of further importance, trans-Saharan trade increased after 100 B.C. with the introduction of the domestic camel from Asia. These developments aided the spread of iron tools and weapons, which had been introduced by the Greeks and Carthaginians in the 700s and 600s B.C. Study the map below and answer the questions that follow.

## Ironworking in Africa

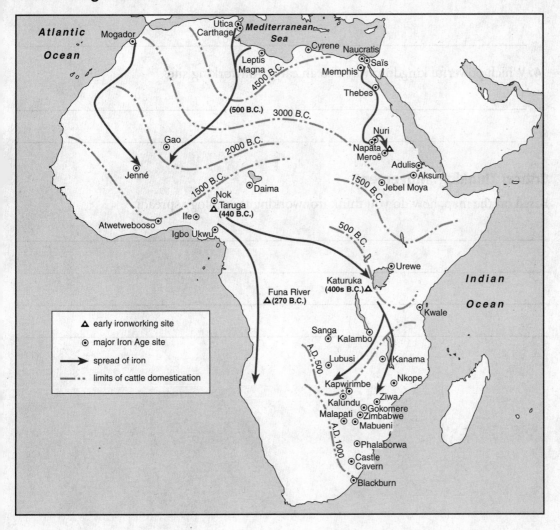

Copyright © by Holt, Rinehart and Winston. All rights reserved.

**1.** To which part of Africa was iron technology first introduced?

_____

_____

**2.** In which direction did iron technology spread?

_____

_____

**3.** What accompanied the introduction of ironworking?

_____

_____

**4.** Which powerful kingdom was also an early ironworking site?

_____

_____

## Critical Thinking: Movement

Based on the map, how do you think ironworking technology spread?

_____

_____

_____

_____

Weeks-Townsend Memorial Library
Union College
Barbourville, KY 40906

Copyright © by Holt, Rinehart and Winston. All rights reserved.